On a
GOLD-BLOOMING
Day
Finding
Fall Treasures

Buffy Silverman

Millbrook Press/Minneapolis

On a **gold-blooming,**

bee-zooming,

sun-dazzling day . . .

Snakes **glide.**

Spiders **hide.**

Crickets **chirp.**

Butterflies **slurp.**

Fluff **lifts.**

Seed **drifts.**

On a **nut-crunching,**

leaf-lunching,

hole-digging day . . .

Clouds **rumble.**

Raindrops **tumble.**

Mushrooms **pop.**

Acorns **drop.**

Fawns **graze.**

Sumacs **blaze.**

On a **frog-leaping**,

log-sleeping,

goose-honking day . . .

Cattails **sway.**

Otters **play.**

Cranes **rattle**.

Fish **skedaddle**.

Muskrats **scoop.**

Swallows **swoop.**

On an **apple-picking,**

seed-sticking,

autumn-colored day . . .

Pumpkins **glow.**

Shadows **grow.**

Woodpeckers **drill.**

Breezes **chill.**

Woolly bears **crawl.**

Leaf piles **call** . . .

Welcome, fall!

What treasures will you find in fall?

As the warm days of summer end, plants and animals prepare for a season of change. Soon the weather will turn cold and food will be harder to find. Plants prepare by growing seeds that can survive until warm weather returns. Some animals store extra food underground. Some begin to eat more. They put on a layer of fat that will fuel them through winter when food is scarce. Some lay eggs that hatch in spring. Others get ready to migrate to places where food is easier to find. Longer nights and cooler weather signal that fall has arrived.

Fall may look different in other areas of the world. The treasures described here are common in the northeastern and midwestern United States. Some can be found all over North America and in other parts of the world.

SNAKES GLIDE

Many snakes that hatch from eggs are youngsters when fall arrives. Young green snakes glide through tall grass, catching insects and spiders. Snakes are on the move in autumn, seeking protected places where they will spend the cold months ahead.

SPIDERS HIDE

It's hard to spot a golden crab spider hidden on a goldenrod flower. This spider doesn't spin a web. Instead, it pounces on insects that visit flowers. Crab spiders can change color to match the flower or leaf where they hide. Their camouflage helps them go undetected by their predators and their prey.

CRICKETS CHIRP

Walk through a field in fall and you will hear *chirp, chirp, chirp*. Male crickets rub their front wings together to chirp. A sharp edge on the underside of one wing scrapes against tiny bumps on the top of the other wing. Female crickets listen for males' chirps to find them. They mate, and the female lays eggs that hatch in spring.

BUTTERFLIES SLURP

A butterfly reaches into flowers with the long tube on its head, called a proboscis. It sucks sweet flower nectar through its proboscis. Monarch butterflies that emerge from their chrysalises in early fall need sugary nectar for energy to fuel their migration to their winter homes. Some monarchs travel 3,000 miles (4,828 km) between their summer and winter homes!

FLUFF LIFTS

Plants cannot move and find a new place to grow. But their seeds can travel. Animals, wind, and water help scatter seeds. Seeds that rely on wind have special structures that help them ride a breeze. A milkweed seed is attached to a fluffy parachute.

SEED DRIFTS

One hundred milkweed seeds can be packed tightly inside its fruit, called a pod. When the pod dries, it splits open. Most seeds drift a short distance and fall to the ground. But some are carried farther. Milkweed seeds sprout when warmth returns in spring.

CLOUDS RUMBLE

Thunderstorms develop when warm air is near the ground and cooler air is above it. Listen for the rumble of thunder on warm days in early autumn. When a lightning bolt travels from a cloud to the ground, it rapidly heats the surrounding air. In less than a second, the air can heat to temperatures five times that of the sun's surface. The heated air expands in every direction creating a large *boom!*

RAINDROPS TUMBLE

Water evaporates from Earth's surface and rises as a gas called water vapor. Vapor condenses into tiny water droplets as it cools in the sky, forming clouds. Inside a cloud, droplets collide, combine, and grow. When droplets become large and heavy, they tumble to the ground as rain.

MUSHROOMS POP

Fungi live in soil year-round. When the ground is wet after rainstorms, fungi send up mushrooms. They seem to appear overnight. Some small mushrooms can grow in a day, rapidly absorbing water. Mushrooms make spores that can grow into new fungi. Wind carries spores, and if they land on soil or wet wood, they begin to grow.

ACORNS DROP

Mature acorns fall from oak trees in late summer and fall. Many animals, such as blue jays, turkeys, raccoons, deer, and wood ducks feast on them. Squirrels, chipmunks, and others bury acorns to eat in winter. Some of these buried acorns never get eaten. Instead, they sprout in spring and grow into new trees.

FAWNS GRAZE

By the time fall begins, fawns no longer drink milk from their mother. They follow her through forests and fields, nibbling grass, twigs, acorns, apples, and mushrooms. This helps them put on fat before winter begins. Soon they will lose their spots and grow a gray coat to blend into the cold winter forest.

SUMACS BLAZE

Sumac leaves are often the first to change color in early autumn. Plant leaves are green because they have a pigment called chlorophyll. Chlorophyll absorbs sunlight. Leaves use the sun's energy to make food. With less sunlight in the fall, leaves stop making food. Chlorophyll breaks down. Then you can see the yellow and orange pigments that were hidden in tree leaves. Some trees also make new red pigments in their leaves.

CATTAILS SWAY

Cattails grow in marshes, along the edges of ponds, and in other wet places. In autumn the plants are topped with brown spikes packed with thousands of seeds. The seed heads fluff out at the end of autumn. Then they look like a cat's fuzzy tail. Wind and water carry the fluff, bringing seeds to new places where they might sprout in spring.

OTTERS PLAY

A river otter slides down a muddy bank and splashes into the water. It paddles with its webbed rear feet, its body snaking through the water. The otter opens its mouth and grabs a slow-swimming fish. Young otters have learned to fish for themselves by fall, but they stay with their families until the next spring.

CRANES RATTLE

Sandhill cranes leave their nesting grounds in late summer and join large flocks. They search for insects and seeds near wetlands and in farmers' fields. As evening arrives, hundreds of cranes flock together in marshy areas where they roost at night. Their loud rattling calls fill the air. As the weather turns colder, many cranes migrate to places where food is more abundant.

FISH SKEDADDLE

Birds, bears, raccoons, people, and many other animals hunt for fish. How do fish avoid their many predators? Often they swim together in a group called a school. A school of fish can confuse a predator, making it more difficult to know where to strike. As one fish turns or speeds up, its neighbors do the same. As the air becomes colder, fish move to deeper, warmer water.

MUSKRATS SCOOP

For many animals, fall is the time to build or repair a home that protects them during winter. Muskrats build lodges. A muskrat scoops and digs with front feet that look like hands. It piles cattails, grasses, and mud to form a mound. Then it digs a burrow beneath the mound.

SWALLOWS SWOOP

Tree swallows twist and turn as they fly through the air, capturing insects. In late summer and early fall, huge flocks of swallows gather together. They start to migrate south where they will find bugs and berries over the winter.

PUMPKINS GLOW

Fall is harvest season. Apples and pears ripen on trees. Farmers dig potatoes from the ground. Pumpkins turn from green to orange, and their skin hardens. They are ready to be cut from long, leafy pumpkin vines. Pumpkin flesh and seeds can be cooked and eaten. Or the seeds can be saved for planting in spring.

SHADOWS GROW

What makes your shadow? Your body blocks sunlight, and a dark shadow forms on the ground. The length of your shadow changes with the seasons. In summer, shadows are shortest because the sun is higher in the sky. Shadows grow in fall when the sun is at a lower angle. They are also longer at sunrise and sunset. That's because your body blocks more light and you cast a longer shadow.

WOODPECKERS DRILL

Imagine slamming your nose and mouth into a tree to get insects that burrow in wood. How do woodpeckers do that without hurting themselves? Shock absorbers in their skull protect their brains. Stiff tail feathers help them balance while their sharp beaks chisel deep into wood. In the fall, woodpeckers chip out several roosting holes where they will sleep in winter. *Tap, tap, tap!*

BREEZES CHILL

When the wind blows against your skin, you might start to shiver. As wind gusts, air molecules bump into your skin. Heat moves from your skin to the air. The moving air carries heat away, and you feel cooler.

WOOLLY BEARS CRAWL

Woolly bear caterpillars are on the move in fall. All summer they have eaten plants and grown. Now they search for a protected spot to spend the winter. Some people say that you can tell how long winter will be by the length of a woolly bear's black bands. But woolly bears can't really predict the weather! They wait for spring to spin a cocoon, and then they become moths.

LEAF PILES CALL

Fall brings changes for plants, animals, and people. Head outside and enjoy the sights and sounds of autumn. What do you notice as summer turns to fall?

Further Reading

Ferry, Beth. *The Scarecrow.* New York: HarperCollins, 2020.

Pak, Kenard. *Goodbye Summer, Hello Autumn.* New York: Henry Holt, 2016.

Paul, Miranda. *Water Is Water: A Book about the Water Cycle.* New York: Roaring Brook, 2015.

Posada, Mia. *Summer Green to Autumn Gold: Uncovering Leaves' Hidden Colors.* Minneapolis: Millbrook Press, 2019.

Rustad, Martha E. H. *Fall Leaves Fun.* Minneapolis: Lerner Publications, 2019.

Sayre, April Pulley. *Full of Fall.* New York: Beach Lane, 2017.

Schaefer, Lola M. *Because of an Acorn.* San Francisco: Chronicle Books, 2016.

Schuh, Mari. *Crayola Fall Colors.* Minneapolis: Lerner Publications, 2018.

Glossary

camouflage: an animal's coloring that blends in with its surroundings

chlorophyll: green pigment in plants that can absorb sunlight

chrysalis: a hard shell that protects a caterpillar as it changes into a butterfly

cocoon: a case of silk that protects a moth caterpillar as it changes into a moth

condense: to change from a gas into a liquid

evaporate: to change from a liquid into a gas

fungi: organisms such as mushrooms that break down dead plants and animals

harvest: the season of the year when ripe crops are gathered

lodge: a home built by a muskrat or beaver

migrate: to move from one region or habitat to another

molecule: the smallest unit of a substance that has all the properties of that substance

pigment: a colored material in plants or animals

predator: an animal that hunts other animals for food

prey: an animal that is hunted and eaten by another animal

proboscis: a long tubelike mouth through which some insects suck their food

roost: a place where birds gather or settle at night

spore: a tiny cell that can grow into a new individual

sumac: a shrub or small tree with leaves that turn bright red in fall

water vapor: water in the form of gas

Photo Acknowledgments

Image credits: Photos by Buffy Silverman, pp. 1, 2, 4 (bottom), 5 (bottom), 11 (top & bottom), 21 (bottom), 24; Rowena K./iStock/Getty Images, p. 3 (top); Kesu01/Getty Images, p. 3 (bottom); Michelle Gilders/Alamy Stock Photo, p. 4 (top); blickwinkel/Alamy Stock Photo, p. 5 (top); SKY Stock/Shutterstock.com, p. 6; jpbcpa/Getty Images, p. 7; Zachary Rathore/Getty Images, p. 8; Ron Sanford/Corbis Documentary/Getty Images, p. 9 (top); Orchidpoet/iStock/Getty Images, p. 9 (bottom); Brad McGinley Photography/Getty Images, p. 10 (top); Steve Satushek/The Image Bank/Getty Images, p. 10 (bottom); Vladimir Ternovoy/Shutterstock.com, p. 12; Olga Shestakova/iStock/Getty Images, p. 13; Jolanta Mosakovska/Shutterstock.com, p. 14; Janet Griffin/Shutterstock.com, p. 15 (top); Manuel ROMARIS/Moment/Getty Images, p. 15 (bottom); Oakland Images/Shutterstock.com, p. 16 (left); David & Micha Sheldon/Alamy Stock Photo, p. 16 (left); Lynn_Bystrom/Getty Images, p. 17 (top); Volodymyr Burdiak/Alamy Stock Photo, p. 17 (bottom); mtruchon/Getty Images, p. 18; Vicki Jauron, Babylon and Beyond Photography/Getty Images, p. 19; kate_sept2004/Getty Images, p. 20; Mieszko9/Getty Images, p. 21 (top); Matej Kotula/500px//Getty Images, p. 22 (left); David Baker - S9Design/Getty Images, p. 22 (right); Maria Jeffs/Getty Images, p. 23 (top); Anita Kot/Getty Images, p. 23 (bottom); LWA/Dann Tardif/Getty Images, p. 25; sun ok/Shutterstock.com, pp. 26–27;

Cover: javarman/Shutterstock.com; Buffy Silverman.

To Emma and Caitlin—wishing you gold-blooming days!

Millbrook Press™
An imprint of Lerner Publishing Group, Inc.
241 First Avenue North
Minneapolis, MN 55401 USA

For reading levels and more information, look up this title at www.lernerbooks.com.

Designed by Emily Harris.

Main body text set in Billy Infant.
Typeface provided by SparkyType.

Library of Congress Cataloging-in-Publication Data

Names: Silverman, Buffy, author.
Title: On a gold-blooming day : finding fall treasures / Buffy Silverman.
Description: Minneapolis : Millbrook Press, [2023] | Includes bibliographical references. | Audience: Ages
    4–9 | Audience: Grades K–1 | Summary: "As autumn begins, plants and animals in nature begin to change
    in all kinds of ways to prepare for winter. Brilliant photos and rhyming text highlight these changes and
    celebrate fall's arrival!"— Provided by publisher.
Identifiers: LCCN 2021052074 (print) | LCCN 2021052075 (ebook) | ISBN 9781728442983 (library binding)
    | ISBN 9781728462677 (ebook)
Subjects: LCSH: Autumn—Juvenile literature. | Seasons—Juvenile literature.
Classification: LCC QB637.7 .S55 2023 (print) | LCC QB637.7 (ebook) | DDC 508.2—dc23/eng/20211126

LC record available at https://lccn.loc.gov/2021052074
LC ebook record available at https://lccn.loc.gov/2021052075

Manufactured in the United States of America
1-50126-49810-2/1/2022